LOVING YOURSELF
ENOUGH TO LIVE:
INSPIRATIONAL MESSAGES FROM
A NEAR DEATH SURVIVOR

KATINA MAKRIS, CCH, CIH

Published by
Hyperspace Internet Technologies, Inc.
1308 Stockton Hill Road, Suite A177
Kingman, AZ 86401
hyperspaceit.com

Library of Congress Control Number:2019912349

ISBN (e-book): 978-0-578-56061-8

ISBN (paperback): 978-0-578-56062-5

ALSO BY KATINA MAKRIS

Out of the Woods: Healing Lyme Disease - Body, Mind and Spirit
USA Book News Finalist award
Autoimmune Illness and Lyme Disease Recovery Guide: Mending
the Body, Mind, and Spirit

Dedication:

For all the seekers in the world
I honor your desire to become the purest form of YOU

CONTENTS

PREFACE   Across the Veil..11

INTRODUCTION 23

Chapter 1   A Forward Path in Healing 27

Chapter 2   The Treasured Gift of this Lifetime 29

Chapter 3   Gratitude Builds Strength.....................................31

Chapter 4   I Recovered from Lyme Disease 33

Chapter 5   Internal Sanctuary 35

Chapter 6   Your Inner Wellspring..37

Chapter 7   Pathway...39

Chapter 8   Moving Through Ups and Downs 41

Chapter 9   Purposeful Mental Images 43

Chapter 10   Your Playground...47

Chapter 11   My First Steps into Tomorrow 49

Chapter 12   Igniting the Spiritual Dimension.......................51

Chapter 13   Grace and Peace...53

Chapter 14   God Bless Us All 55

Chapter 15   Align Your Inner Healing Resources..................57

Chapter 16   Believe and See...59

Chapter 17   Day by Day 61

Chapter 18   May We Be Graced 63

Chapter 19   The Void 65

Chapter 20   May We Embrace Our Purpose 67

Chapter 21   Be Filled with Light..69

Chapter 22   Working from Our Highest Good 71

Chapter 23   Optimal Health in a Stormy Crossing 73

Chapter 24   11:11...75

Chapter 25   Courage to be Whole...77

Chapter 26   Truth 79

Chapter 27   Life with a Mission 81

Chapter 28   Healing Happens on the Inside...........................83

Chapter 29   Deep Rest 85

Chapter 30   Passageway Through Change................................87

Chapter 31   Spirit Calling for Change.....................................89

Chapter 32   Your Most Powerful Ally 93

Chapter 33   Tending a Broken Spirit 95

Chapter 34   Deep Journey...97

Chapter 35   All is Possible...99

Chapter 36   Thriving Versus Surviving 101

Chapter 37   Thunderstorm of Change 103

Chapter 38   The Lesson of Character 105

Chapter 39   Resiliency 107

Chapter 40   Your Spirit is Mighty 109

Chapter 41   Blessed to Be 111

Chapter 42   Comfort and Inspiration......................................113

Chapter 43   Dispel the Blocks..115

Chapter 44   Tapping Life Force 117

Chapter 45 The Labyrinth...119

Chapter 46 You are Miraculous................................123

Chapter 47 To Be Summoned 125

Chapter 48 See Beyond the Suffering......................127

Chapter 49 Power of Will...129

Chapter 50 Your Test..131

Chapter 51 Here on Purpose 133

Chapter 52 Freedom to Expand 135

Chapter 53 Accept Change 137

Chapter 54 The Quest...139

Chapter 55 Harness Your Belief 141

Chapter 56 Phoenix Rising.......................................143

Chapter 57 Today I Am Stronger 145

Chapter 58 The Soothsayer.......................................147

Chapter 59 In Parting 153

ABOUT THE AUTHOR 155

ACKNOWLEDGEMENTS...157

PREFACE

Across the Veil

I lie flat as a railway bed for month after month, throughout the humid summer of 2005. Too weak to lift my head for more than a few minutes at a time, I manage being vertical for only the most directed necessities: a trip to the bathroom, sitting up to eat, changing my clothes. As dawn breaks, Hunter stirs me from under my heavy, sodden sleep with a breakfast tray of eggs, juice and toast. My son, in his eight-year-old zest, crawls atop my bed for a pre-camp kiss, then flits out the door for his freewheeling day.

The air conditioners drone, the house lays still, like a lion lounging in the heat of the African plains. Outside the silent windows, I see the sun blazing, the hollyhocks climbing, the heat mounting. All I can manage is a rotation of position, from left side to right and then over supine onto my back. Faithfully, each day, I force myself out of my bed and pajamas. If I linger too long in either, my spirits flag so deeply into a plummeting trench of despair and fear, that it's close to impossible to fathom a return to wellness. Months into this recent nosedive, I'm self-trained to avoid emotional or psychic influences triggering deepening depression, after five years of chronic debilitating illness.

I slide down the stairs, propping myself on the oak handrail, diving directly onto the waiting sofa, managing to flick on the

CD player *en route*. The same five discs have been playing round and round for two months now, daily. Hours on end, the chords and harmonies waft around my cotton filled head, soothing my jangled nerves and trembling limbs.

I answer no phones, look at no TV, turn on no computers, read nothing, my cognitive function has been destroyed. The early onset dementia symptoms prevent me from even recalling words to make a grocery list.

I'm in a vacuum, detached from the world, its bustling societal activities, political happenings, and even trends in the weather. All day, alone and motionless, I wrestle instead with my own seismic quakes and shifts. I can handle nothing more.

I proclaim myself a hothouse plant, as any minor external fluctuation can send me into a completely disharmonious flux. Direct sunlight, a five-degree temperature shift, the air conditioner drafting on me, the wrong pillow, a slamming door are all aggravating. I hate it. I'm beyond catlike finicky. I feel as if I've been taken hostage by my malingering body. It blows my mind really. Formerly vital, athletic, spontaneous and even occasionally reckless, now I'm in a state of captive restraint and stillness.

I've never before known how to be this still. I start to think about loneliness and death and the possibility of true miracles. In these decaying times I become acquainted with parts of myself I never knew existed. It's as if I'm discovering a piece of terrain in the vast tableau of the universe in which I occupy less than a nanosecond of importance. These conceptual facts feel daunting and spectral in a sense. My insignificance begins to take precedence in my thought patterns.

Who am I really?

Why am I even here?

After the hundreds I have helped heal in my homeopathic practice why can no one, in western or holistic medicine help me?

I cry a lot, long, heaving sobs that clench my stomach muscles. At night, I cry quiet, self-pitying tears, drowning in the abyss of my own unknown—the unknown of this mysterious illness, of my future, of my conscious and unconscious minds. A part of me is close to giving up hope. But I cling desperately to a very tiny flicker of inner knowing that I will not give up. Having spent so much of my life in Natural Medicine, I deeply trust there are ways, maybe yet unclear to me, that will help my body right itself and start to heal. I refuse to give up on that belief.

I rummage through my thoughts and feelings, thinking of so many novels and poems cataloging deaths resulting from sadness. The despair, the depression, the overwhelming grief within breaks these characters' beings, their will, their ability to breathe and live in a normal sense. They die. I have seen the elderly loose hope and die, after the death of a beloved spouse. To die from sadness.

Will I, too, die now? Am I literally dying? Some days I really grapple with this notion. Is this a terminal illness? Is it a disease not yet captured on film or lab testing? These numbing limbs and flopping feet feel like MS in a way. Maybe Lou Gehrig's disease? But the seventeen Neurologists at prominent New England hospitals have confirmed that I have no neurological disease process. The kidney specialist and oncologists say I do not have a cancer. The Internists say that my GI trouble is Irritable Bowel Syndrome and that the Esptein-Barr titers are once again high. But why? Thousands of dollars later, scans and scopes *ad infinitum*, I lie pallid and inert, like a lifeless brook trout no longer even able to flail or flop a silvery fin.

This is surreal for one of the most elite Homeopathic practitioners in the USA to fall so tragically ill and to have lost all that I built in my life; illustrious career, savings, marriage, home, family and identity all stripped from me. I am heartbroken. But there is nothing more to do but to rest and wait, take my vitamins and homeopathic remedies, see the acupuncturist. I pray…but I am close to giving up.

I call my father, wailing into the phone. "I'm so weak. I don't think I'll ever get well."

My eternally optimistic, strong to the very marrow of the soul father will not let me give up. Having fought back from three near death experiences, white light and all, during his eighty years on earth, he gives me another of his famous pep talks.

"You can do it, Katina. Hang in there. You're strong, very strong. Don't forget you are a Makris. We're tough, Black Sea Greeks. There's nothing you can't overcome. Use your will, Sweetheart. Use your will. Think of a beautiful place you love. Use it as a way to soothe your mind and promote healthy brain waves. Don't forget you have a young son you need to raise and be there for. No one but you can give him the tender loving care that only you so perfectly know how to show. Please Sweetheart, know that you can do this. Be patient. Look at all that I beat out, even when they told me I would die! Medical science is negative, you must be only positive."

I continue to whimper, but I listen to him, as I always have when in trouble. My father is right, always right about the big things in life. He's a stunning man, gifted with so much wisdom, integrity, and a will of proportions rarely glimpsed in life. Having been left to die in the trenches of the Philippines in WWII, he was found by medics days later and managed to rally from a broken back, shrapnel blinding his one eye, crystallized kidneys, and more. I saw him beat out encephalitis, mumps, and embolisms in my youth. If he could do those things, then certainly I can hang on through this collapse. He's right. I need to reach in and draw on my will, but it feels so flimsy and flaccid.

I realize, though, in these moments, that I am dying a death of sorts. It's a spiritual death. I sense that this illness, this time of retreat from the world, is forcing me to self-examine, to let go of ways of being and living—even ways of relating—that are not best for me. It was hard to really look at this sort of thing when I was so busy living full tilt in the world. I always gobbled up life, did one hundred and twelve things in a day, ran two offices, taught classes, wrote my newspaper health column, sat on the national homeopathic council board, kept the household in motion, traveled, partied, tended the organic garden, reared the kids, adored my husband. Stepping off the hamster wheel, I see how hastily I lived my life. And, I loved it!

This illness is asking a lot of me. It's asking me to change so much of my template. It feels right now like all it wants me to do is give up. Give over my varied ways of living my life, knowing myself, sharing with others. I'm at the very edge of myself. Something essential to my soul feels like it's starting to separate from me, like I'm moving away from my own body.

Lying on the green floral sofa, its back against my home's north wall, I gaze across the cherry floors to the low-slung windows wreathed in summer sunshine. My misery is overwhelming. My heart is not beating properly. It is skipping and dropping. My breathing is so shallow. I feel my spirit — or is it myself? — start to lift from my body. I close my eyes and sense I'm taking flight of sorts. I'm leaving. Where am I going?

Is this death?

With my eyes closed, my forehead is filling with a picture. It's as if a vivid movie is running in my head. I watch it with great intent. I feel myself floating over the house, looking down on the roof, then inside, glimpsing my weakened form lying listless on the couch, long brown hair draped down my back. I have feelings of sympathy and tenderness for my own self, so wretchedly ill.

With that I turn my vision north, up the road we live on. I'm gazing above the tall, leafy oaks and bristling white pines toward the string of power lines that lie ahead. I become aware that I'm flying, hovering over the trees and heading along the power lines, over the granite rock cropping toward the bluing sky and the hills of the neighboring township of Hancock.

"Oh my God. I'm flying. My spirit has taken flight," I realize.

With that, I have a profound awareness that I'm not alone. To my right, just off my shoulder, is a grand and stately bald eagle, its snow-capped head beaming in the sunlight. His broad brown wings stretch wide, beating with great strength and grace. I'm filled with awe as I feel this powerful bird so close to me. As if in a dance, the eagle dips to its left, slipping right under me. The next thing I know we're flying together in tandem, me lying on his shoulders and back, my arms outstretched along his wings. In some nonverbal way the eagle communicates to me. Words, sentences, feelings arise in my consciousness as if uttered by the glorious creature. I listen internally with rapt attention.

"I'm your ally, Katina. We will fly together now and forever. Trust in my strength and my guidance. I will not let you down. But, in turn, you must trust in yourself, in your own wisdom and intuition, for it's very powerful. This time in your life has been a trial, a test of your inner strength. You have shown great courage and determination in a time of great darkness these past five years. You are learning to master the trickery of the mind, the demons that prey on one's soul, the trappings of emotions. I will be with you now, Katina. You have earned your rights of vision. You have been given the gift of eagle's wings. Come soar with me. We will touch the lives of others. Open yourself to the doorway of the divine. You are on the cusp of new understandings. I will be your guide. You can die now or choose to have faith in me."

I don't know what to think. It seems so fantastical and natural at the same time. My life is so ransacked, with nothing else left to lose. I nod *Yes* to the eagle, surrendering to his knowing.

Riding high in the summer sky, we fly over my favorite sequestered pond, deep in the uninhabited woods. I see the sunshine dancing on the crystal water, the leaves shimmying in the warm breeze. My heart fills as we crest the ridge of Lake Nubanuist and circle Spoonwood Pond where my husband and I camped often with the children, swimming so joyfully at the Old Yeller rope swing.

I spy a twiggy nest resting in the topmost limbs of a towering tree. I notice a young, mottled eagle resting inside, its eyes blinking as our sweeping shadow skims by. I sense that this is the nest and baby of my newfound eagle ally. It's all stunningly beautiful, pixel perfect, and anointed with a spell of divinity and magic. In these moments of unheralded vision, I am spellbound.

Eventually, we circle to the west and south, flying for my own home, passing over familiar farms and schools, valleys and back roads. I manage to pick out all of the other residences in which I have dwelt during my time up here in New Hampshire. It's like a summation of fourteen years. I can see the big picture of my history.

Am I dreaming or is this a vision or hallucination?

But the majestic bird is strong and warm to my touch. His feathers are thick and downy as I clutch to him in flight. He is so strong!

The eagle drops down close to the pine tops of the woods behind my home. As we approach my pinprick of a yard, he slows down slightly and turns his head to the left, so I look right into his clear marble like eye. I see inside his spirit to his soul. Oddly, I feel an intelligent being in there. He is familiar to me in some curious way. His presence is powerful. Then suddenly, my eagle is gone just as mysteriously as he appeared, in a rapid wing beat of surprise.

I hastily descend back into my body lying on the sofa. It hurts something fierce when I land. Every bone and body part feel jolted, like I fell on cement!

"Home, I'm home," I say, stunned and wildly curious about what has just happened to me. Was that an angel, a spirit guide, a shamanic journey or a near death experience? I am stunned and too afraid to even try to move.

I feel a quiet peace and a strange sense of contentedness. It's as if on my journey with the eagle, I've gained an awareness that if I can stay attuned to my higher power, to divinity, to what people know as God, and not be trapped in the morass of my emotions, I'll find my way out of this snarl of illness. Direction will come to me; answers will be found.

And surely enough, the answers funneled in rapidly after this levitation from my body, into the unseen realm and in concert with this spiritual guide, which I know think of as my animal totem. Within two weeks of 'serendipitous' occurrences, I was sitting in the office of a brilliant Ph.D., Clinical Nutritionist colleague in my wheelchair, feeling sorry for myself and grateful that Dr. Jeff had a clear idea of what made a vibrant, holistic practitioner and lifestyle specimen deteriorate in her 40's to a broken invalid: Lyme disease, an infectious bacterial illness transmitted by a tiny insect- the tick!

I was never so elated and furious simultaneously, when the specialty testing laboratory proved that yes, *burgdorferi b.* was occupying my body in heavy encampment (in spite of the three false negative findings from traditional national labs over the years and misdiagnosis) and that numerous of my systems were damaged and depleted: gut, heart, brain and nerves, muscles and more. The doctor outlined a complete protocol which eventually helped me to heal fully and not suffer with consequences. It was a two to three years estimate to return to 80% of my former self and man, was I determined, after five years of extreme pain, collapse and suffering were validated and no longer shuffled off as being perimenopause, autoimmune illnesses or hypochondria, that I could heal. Lyme disease is a devastating disease when misdiagnosed and improperly treated in the early weeks of infection. I was a full-blown case of medical mismanagement yet was willfully set on full recovery now that I understood what had stricken me.

The remarkable news is that I did recover, and beyond the 80% to 100%. I started to not discount my intuition, I followed the natural medicine protocols to a "t" over a five-year period and most profoundly I recognized it was just as critical I focus on my broken spirit as well as my broken body. With the eagle's message to trust my instincts, I 'coincidentally' united with a renowned spiritual teacher and healer, Dr. Meredith Young Sowers, who encouraged me to attend her yearlong spiritual intuitive certification training. Still horizontal most all day, I had no idea how I could manage these one weeklong quarterly on location modules, nor the weekly phone classes and homework. But, my deep desire to heal and reclaim a life, forced me to bite down hard, commit and have inner faith I could pull this off somehow. It all worked! (I detail the recovery story in my award-winning memoir, "Out of The Woods, Healing Lyme Disease, Body, Mind & Spirit", Skyhorse Publishing).

I must say my spiritual awakening and near-death experience have changed me forever, all in good ways. I returned to homeopathic practice eventually, now devoting my skills solely to chronic Lyme and autoimmune disease cases. I published two books within four years and went out on the road into the heart of the Lyme disease epidemic and taught at over 195 events, ranging from support groups, libraries, major international health conferences and becoming a workshop leader, in less than seven years' time. A stunning jewel was that I was culled to host a cutting edge weekly live radio program, *"Lyme Light Radio with Katina"* on a global 600 station syndicate. My program was their fastest growing one in a decade, with 2 million tracked listeners as its' peak, as I interviewed the world's most contemporary researchers, physicians, foundation leaders and other recoveree cases. The breadth of my new life rebirth was as broad reaching and powerful as that mighty eagle's wingspan.

So often, I am in awe of my personal transformation at the hand of a treacherous, deadly disease, and that somehow I became anointed to carry forth as a messenger, Inspirational Speaker and a living testimony to the power of the human mind and the deep wellspring of inner powers we bear, if we can only learn how to tap into them. They are our birthrights. The key is coming to practice self-love in a vastly over externalized society of quick feeds and fixes, and to spend time daily cultivating your inner Garden of Eden of personal powers and belief.

With this awareness in mind, after working with literally thousands of emotionally, physically, mentally and spiritually suffering folks in the past decade, I have become conscious of just how much nurturing our culture needs in the form of insightful guidance, daily reminders and inspirational wisdom to help find our own path to both happiness and healing.

The result is this simple, yet timely book of inspired messages that move through me as a near death survivor and seasoned healer. Those of us who cross over to the 'other side', leave our body at a near death juncture and are graced with the uncommon opportunity to meet a benevolent spirit guide, communicate with a deceased ancestor, or are touched by God or an angel of mercy, and return to the light and living with more than a renewed lease on life, but often with either increased energetic accessibility to the unseen realm, enhanced healing properties, a frank mission of passion, and/or the ability to thrive in such ways that we bring some gift of altruistic service to mankind.

I am deeply blessed, forever graced with guidance from the unseen and believe wholeheartedly that my life is not random but has been completely charted to carry forth my enhanced healing power and gift of communication. Nine years fully well and thriving now in so many ways, my ever understanding and perceptive editor, Robbi Gunter has encouraged me to share some of the 'pearls' of my teachings, journal entries, keynote speech inspirations and messages from across the veil with you.

People like me are still as human as all, yet often, our cross-over experience, as well as the extremely disciplined years of personal devotion to mending body, mind and spirit, tally up a treasure trove of human understanding and inspired understandings that are motivational messages to accepting change and embracing your ultimate life process of personal growth.

May these pages ahead help you to believe in yourself and that nothing really is impossible. Our mind, heart and spirit are vastly capable and when we take the time to be quiet and present within our self, versus multitasking and pushing so hard on the external planes of societal expectations. Often, we can become disconnected or fuzzy in our connection to inner source and higher consciousness. My intention is to help illuminate your pathway of inner resource.

I hope to share thoughts and insights and messages of inspiration to many of you on your healing journey or merely daily life of more aware living. As both a seeker and a messenger, I look forward to sharing in mutual support, the amazing gifts of inner mind-body-spirit skills we all possess.

With blessings,
Katina Makris, CCH, CIH
2019

INTRODUCTION

What would you do if the things that mattered most to you in life were suddenly torn away? Most of us would experience shock and bewilderment. Loss of health, relationships, family, financial stability, status, home, country…the list goes on. When it happens, we are shrouded with uncertainty.

One of the most frightening things to lose is health. When you are vibrant and active, to have your body completely fail can be devastating. The inability to do normal activities, such as go to work, care for your family or even get out of bed to walk a few steps is beyond comprehension for most of us. We take it for granted that no matter what else is going down the tubes, we can still function physically.

Katina Makris faced the unthinkable. She had worked hard to build a thriving homeopathic practice of two decades, reared her loving family and cherished the comfort of her peaceful country home. Without warning, she was hit hard with violent flu symptoms, vertigo, intense sweats and swollen glands. Her illness was relentless and caused her to suffer terribly. Many years would pass before she was finally diagnosed with neurological Lyme disease. In the meantime, she lost everything that made up her treasured world. Eventually, the cruel disease laid her down on her deathbed.

As Katina lay helpless, succumbing to the devastating effects of Lyme disease, something inside her stirred. She realized she had a choice. Her body was quickly draining of life force, but her mind and spirit were strong. She made a conscious decision to come back to the living, knowing deep in her being that she had something more to offer the world. Despite the odds, which were heavily against her, she dedicated herself daily to her recovery, using sheer willpower and inner belief to win the battles along the way.

During her healing journey, Katina recognized the critical component of mending her broken spirit along with her broken body. She applied and was accepted at The Stillpoint School of Integrative Life Healing where she was certified as a spiritual healer and was class valedictorian.

Katina experienced recovery from Lyme disease using only natural healing protocols. She applied what she learned to heal others. She became a teacher and international speaker. She authored two great books – *Out of the Woods: Healing from Lyme Disease for Body, Mind and Spirit* and *Autoimmune Illness and Lyme Disease Recovery Guide*. She became the U.S. international spokesperson for Lyme disease and keynote speaker for the Ticked Off Music Festivals and other Lyme disease rallies and fundraisers. Her workshops venues soared to standing room only, including prestigious venues like Omega Institute, Art of Living, The Dean Center at Mass General Hospital and more.

For Katina, recovering from a serious illness became a personal quest and transformation. She gained insight into the workings of her own mind. It became evident that she must maintain a strict vigilance over her thoughts and focus on the positive outcome. As she traveled the world teaching about Lyme disease and the importance of Integrative Medicine in America's lopsided health care model, her compassion grew for the people she met. More than anything, she wanted to show them the way out of their suffering. She began sharing her innermost thoughts and feelings, desiring to provide light in the darkness.

This book is a compilation of Katina's most poignant journal entries. They illustrate the struggles she faced as she progressed through her recovery. They reveal the deep self-love and love for others that became the motivating force in her life. This book is for anyone that has suffered loss or confusion. In those moments when you feel like you just cannot go on, she provides comfort and encouragement. Like her personal symbol, the starfish, Katina's words wrap you in infinite divine love. Each time you turn the page, know she is guiding you vigilantly, using her brilliance and intuition to inspire.

Take your time in reading Katina's messages. Perhaps start your own journal, too, as a way to enter your own 'Garden of Eden' that Katina portrays. She will help you hone your inner willpower, vision and self-love by taking the time to digest her very pure and powerful insights. Near death survivors truly are a special breed. Having 'touched' the other side, we find a soul like Katina's has chosen to come back to all of us for more than purely selfish reasons. I find I am constantly moved at a very deep level by her touching words of wisdom and everlasting loving grace.

It is my honor to be Katina's friend. I believe you will discover in these pages, that she is your spiritual friend and teacher, too. This is a book for us all, in sickness and in health. Thank you, Katina.

Robbi Gunter
2019

1

A Forward Path in Healing

Today and tomorrow I honor the strength and willpower so many of us need to lean on, in order to find a forward path in healing.

2

THE TREASURED GIFT
OF THIS LIFETIME

I am taking a brief moment to send my deep healing wishes to
all those who suffer with illness in their life. I know the pains,
the sorrow, the isolation, the fears and the dependency it can
create in your world. Having been bed ridden and house bound
for many years myself, I recall the loneliness and confusion I
often felt. I missed the comings and goings of just everyday
happenings, like driving or going out sledding with my kids.
Using my body in an athletic way was a huge loss for me and
I pined to swim in the surf or dance all sweaty hot in a dimly
lit music filled bar. I loved cooking and gardening and hiking
in the pine clad forests. Working in my busy office, tending to
the woes of little ones and their ear infections of the misery of
menstrual discomforts among the womenfolk, slipped away as

29

the *undiagnosed* Lyme disease eroded my world, stripping me of so very much.

I am a new person now. Five years of devoted healing work helped me reclaim my life in a vibrant new vibration. I know many of you have been stymied by the medical profession, as you try to recover from the physical woes. This creates much confusion and a sense of betrayal for some of us. Healing requires both physical ministering, personal care and inner poise. Please know that you are gifted and wise and sensing beings.

There are personal tools and energies we can each harness and use to help ourselves promote a shift in our health and well-being. By using positive intention, prayers for healing, willpower statements, you can initiate a trickle of the feel-good hormones and neurotransmitters in the brain, which will stimulate the immune system. Dancing and laughing in glee last weekend reminded me of what joy and passion we possess within, so accessible via music, art, comedy and beauty.

So, let's take a break. Let's turn off the lights, stoke the fire, and put on some great music. Allow your mind to wander, your eyes to drift, your skin to sense. Just hang out. It's Ok. Actually, it is wonderful. Daydreams, leisurely talks, gazing at the autumn leaves are gestures of self-nourishment. Appreciate your senses, the color of the sky, the energy of a moment. You are feeding your spirit when you hang out in this void of space-the act of not doing, but just *being.*

So, beautiful beings, my new friends and acquaintances, readers and maybe just passers-by, I remind you all, to cherish the pleasure, the bounty, the grace of just simply *being* you! In the moment of such stillness may you glimpse the treasured gift of this lifetime.

3

GRATITUDE BUILDS STRENGTH

I am blessed. I feel deep respect for the precious gift of renewal. Take a moment to feel and reflect on a moment of grace or beauty in the past year. It can be a touchstone of sorts to return to in a troubled patch. Gratitude builds strength.

4

I RECOVERED FROM LYME DISEASE

I recovered from advanced chronic Lyme completely. Working diligently with naturopathic medicine (herbs), acupuncture, homeopathy and a very seasoned clinical nutritionist, to rebuild my depleted and damaged bodily systems, were the essential pieces to help me to recover. It was five solid years of devoted work.

5

INTERNAL SANCTUARY

It is remarkable for me to say, that because of my Lyme disease experience, I have grown in spiritual depth and breadth. I have created my own internal sanctuary.

6

YOUR INNER WELLSPRING

I learned how to successfully move within, toward my SELF. The inner riches and skills I developed, which in turn prompted a healing at a deeper, more energetic and cellular level, happened ONLY because of this path I took towards my soul's center. It is with great reverence, I now personally care for this treasured space within, and the energy that it exemplifies.

It is a tricky juggling act, one I manage with alert consciousness daily, to avoid being drawn, pulled, stretched excessively by the busyness, demands, schedules, details of the exciting and sometimes overwhelming opportunities of the outer world, we so rampantly work and play in. I like it out there, I admit. As an extrovert, people lover and excitement "junkie" of yore, it is easy for me to be seduced by the amazing colors, feelings, events swirling around me constantly; the internet, media activities fueling it all exponentially.

And yet, I KNOW how essential it is I nurture and preserve my inner spiritual life. To be full and healthy, I need to tend to the wellspring. Meditation, alone time, gratuities, creativity, beauty, personal blessings and intentions are my daily gestures for renewal, helping me follow Buddha's message of life, light, and love. I am not a practicing Buddhist, *per se*, however, his messages that I read or glean, often resonate with a certain truth I just "get."

I hope you can take this offering of mine as a reminder to honor and nurture your own inner wellspring and sanctuary. You are too precious to neglect.

7

PATHWAY

I love the word pathway. "Pathway" suggests a trail to me. Not a blazed, trampled one, but instead one that is evocative and maybe even secret or discrete. Likewise, a pathway gives me a direction. It suggests a way to go; a known route to a destination. Those marked hiking trails up mountainsides maintain distinct progress, as step by step you ascend to the summit, worn roots and knobby boulders passed over by others before you. The path is reassuring—in fact, it is an intricate map of sorts.

A pathway of particular interest and great regenerating capacity is the invisible one working between our mind and body. The entire human body is not randomly designed. Joy and sorrow favor the lungs, indignation the gallbladder. Metaphysics studies this interplay. Coming to understand these interrelationships puts an extremely different posture on doctoring, as there are more influences to affect change and cure than just externally directed modalities. Humans bear inner powers and use of the mind is a prominent player.

The art of stillness, creativity, will, affirmation, intention, meditation, and prayer all have intrinsic roles. These personal powers are natural and free and all yours. You do not have to pay someone for these healing services, you merely must practice them faithfully and with care, because reinforcement on a daily basis is what will translate to cellular change at the physiological level, enabling you to transform a condition, state, or symptoms.

You have the power. Just as the map of a hiking trail serves the hiker, I will guide you on the mind-body pathway. Igniting this circuit is not that difficult once you understand. The work is in finding clarity within yourself, making a commitment, and persisting with daily practice. Take the time to make notes, journal, sketch, sing, write music, corral your discoveries. In time you will find answers to many of your confusions and questions within your own words, discoveries and processing of emotions these messages may stimulate.

8

MOVING THROUGH UPS
AND DOWNS

L ife is a Ferris wheel of ups and downs, circling around in everlasting cycles, the seasons remind us of the changes. Yet often we human beings do not honor the wisdom of nature and instead PUSH through the time-honored ups and downs, the ins and outs, forcing ourselves to keep moving, doing and achieving.

I know this pattern of defying natural rhythms, I too pushed too far. The result was a very long bout of chronic autoimmune style illness. Though Lyme disease removed me from the outer world and all I loved, it also showed me many miracles. In fact, my ten-year healing journey was nothing short of profound!

9

PURPOSEFUL MENTAL IMAGES

B
y no stretch of the imagination or words, I can say that I was so wretchedly ill, that death was close at hand, and others used the term "critical," as I lay bedridden, too weak to dress or shower on my own. Dementia symptoms had set in, palsy tremors and nightmarish anxiety and obsessive thought patterns ran rampant, making me feel honestly, insane. My mind and body were horrifically ravaged. Lyme disease can be so frightening.

I was determined to be well and reclaim my life completely. Being half-way well was not going to be satisfactory for me. Soon I was being presented with the challenge of being patient with convalescence, yet also not slumping or settling for getting just part-way better.

To outsiders this may sound like nonsense, but to a 'Lymie', well you know just what I am talking about. It is a delicate balancing act to accept a moderate, slow paced path to recovery and to not just flag into couch potato, sluggish stasis. It is that final push, the steepest part of the ascent to the summit, that is often the most grueling phase in a high mountain trek. For me, this is no different with overcoming chronic Lyme disease. After a long, arduous, often muddy course, switchbacks included, holding on and forging to the uninhabited, rock bare summit is a victory!

Much of the chronic illness or cancer conquest involves a positive mental mindset and use of willpower. Developing inner strength and patience clearly are helpmates. But, the piece actually of greatest assistance to me during the "final summit" of "Mount Lyme," involved creating an inner sanctuary within my being. Stilling my overactive mind, letting go of the negative mental Lyme vortex and truly cherishing my own sensitivity was a critical turning point. Like a rope belay over a rocky face, this inner sanctuary is an oasis in the storm of any illness, and an essential supportive measure if one wishes to reach the pinnacle of full recovery.

Purposefully setting positive mental images in our mind's eye is the first step in creating an inner sanctuary. I urge you to see yourself in your own happy, comfortable, healthy setting. Really sit with this image; your eyes closed, seeing the colors, sensing the smells and textures. Be there! Allow your physical and emotional self to relish in this positive setting and feelings. In doing so, you are initiating the mind-body healing pathway, and beginning to produce a trickle of hormones and neurochemicals that are the beneficial variety and will in turn stimulate the immune system.

I suggest visiting this lovely place within your mind's eye, many times in your day, reinforcing a positive trend. By cultivating this inner sanctuary of comfort and beauty, you are accessing your own healing energy and intention to embrace wellness. All forms of illness or loss of well-being can benefit from working with our own inner healing powers.

May you be graced with peace and beauty, as you began to create your own inner sanctuary.

10

YOUR PLAYGROUND

The entire world is your playground. You can achieve anything you want in this lifetime! I feel proud and honored to be living now and sharing my words with others. How remarkable my journey has been! Lyme stripped me of everything I cherished. But I worked hard to recover, and now my internal awareness and hard-earned rewards are enduring. I get to pay it forward now.

11

MY FIRST STEPS INTO TOMORROW

Today, I take my first steps into tomorrow. I reach way deep down inside into the core of my being. From the pit of my belly I draw forth my formerly sagging will. Making a personal pact of intention, I close my eyes and see myself standing upright and strong like a broad-reaching copper beech tree. I'm smiling and radiant. I look and feel healthy and strong, confident and happy, successful and powerful.

I will heal completely, I tell myself. I will beat the Lyme disease. I will regain my health, strength, and stamina and be whole, happy, and successful. Starting now I leave the past behind and step into a new and better future. I will be guarded and protected.

From today forward I begin to recite my pact of intention each day in my morning meditation, at first prone on the sofa, then sitting, and eventually standing. I refuse to slip back into the downward spiral of all the cataclysmic tailspins over the past five grueling years. I'm determined to heal. No one will stop me. It will be.

May your healing journeys bring you to the close concert of inner resources I discovered. Willpower, intention, faith, self-belief, love and openness can create room for change and healing. I send you strength and generosity.

12

IGNITING THE
SPIRITUAL DIMENSION

If I keep speaking and teaching, sharing and writing, I
believe each droplet of goodwill and effort I lend will
affect the winds of change. A momentum will build as we
coalesce. Group synergy can build a web of community and
compassion. My intention to ignite the spiritual dimension of
healing in each individual, can in turn stir great healing energy
within and without. Over time and in process, the tides will
shift!

I pray that in my lifetime I will witness an end to the
Lyme disease epidemic. The abysmal weakness, the pains, the
isolation, the confusion, the losses will be replaced with buoyant
joy, vibrant energy, abundant creativity, a caring stewardship

of Earth and a return to play and freedom among nature- my temple of solace.

As evening settles in, I light the candles, I sit still, listening to the winter winds whisking in on a distant tremolo. Soon the snows will arrive, blanketing us in whiteness and I will turn within; a time of meditations, writings and contemplation for me.

At this threshold of transition, I bow to each of the four directions. To the East, I offer my thanks for the vibrant, fresh energy that propelled me far and wide this year. To the South, I offer gratitude for feeding me so fully with love and acceptance, joy and sharing on each of my ventures. To the West, I acknowledge your mighty energy of fortitude and endurance to hold me, as I pushed myself physically like I was a youngster. To the North, I offer my pure respect for your guidance and perfect patience, bringing me home safely each trip and always gracing me with wisdom.

I have been moved deeply by all that I've experienced in this magical year. May my work and efforts bring the ministering of hope and inspiration I aimed for.

13

GRACE AND PEACE

I ask for grace. I ask for peace. I ask for safety, trust and faith. May there be love in our hearts. May we each let go of that which binds or wounds us and turn towards the sun and beckon in all that breathes life and joy into our souls.

14

GOD BLESS US ALL

Reaching for a cart, I backed up and brushed the heel of an elderly woman leaving with her bags of food. A mere brush of my shoe and somehow, she went into stock still frozen mode. I moved ahead and then glanced back...She remained frozen. I turned and went back to check on her, sensing something was wrong.

"Are you ok?" I ask.

"No. I have a back problem and now am in pain," an icy voice and stony glare ahead, not at me.

"I am sorry. I know about pain. Can I help you in some way?" I offer.

"No. No one can help me," the tone is like cement.

"Should I help you wheel your cart?"

"No."

"I am sorry. I didn't mean to hurt you. My foot just skimmed by your heel," my sensing words express.

Stillness…no words, no eye contact.

I weave my energy from my heart towards hers…I stay still, too.

She looks at me oddly. I smile. She glowers.

"I hope you have a Merry Christmas," I suggest.

"Not possible," she mumbles.

Am I daunted? Am I put off? A bit. Then a thought arises in me. Her cart is shallow in groceries compared to the others. Maybe she is alone?

"So, do you have family to help you?"

"No."

It was then that I felt her pain, more than the back or than the shoe skimming. It was the pain of loneliness. I knew that feeling.

I then heard odd words coming from me. "Well, I hope the spirit of your ancestors visit you this holiday. They can be a sort of company, maybe?"

"Yes. I have already lit the candles for them," the crackled woman says.

Finally, her eyes meet mine. I see the weariness in her soul.

I smile. She tries to. I nod. She moves on, and I hear very faintly. "God bless."

Motionless, I absorb this moment of grace. I turn and enter the maze of aisles. The holiday freneticism throngs, yet a quiet pool sits in my chest. Two unsuspect strangers threaded with a simple gift today, that of human compassion.

God bless us all, alone, in company, in comfort, in peace, in need, in joy. It is the gift of the heart that touches most simply.

15

ALIGN YOUR INNER HEALING RESOURCES

I vowed to myself on my sickbed that *when* I recovered, I would do what I felt moved me and hold nothing back. A channel opened in me, I felt it one day when in deep meditation. Energy flooded in my crown chakra. I knew then that I was meant to move forward and live on purpose, not by accident or by default, but with clear intention and with heart. Some days I feel lit from within. I can't hold my energy back. I let it flow; writing, counselling, you name it, and I won't suppress it.

I feel graced by this life and my path. I take nothing for granted and walk it with profound thanks and in pride.

The Lyme Disease ordeal was horrific, but ultimately a journey of personal transformation. Out the other side now, ignited within by my intention to help others find ways to transform their own suffering into rebirth, I know there is no possible way to go back to the old me, the conditioned one, the less conscious one, the over-tasking one. Fueled by spirit, ignited by love, moved by the powers of transformation, I want to encourage those of you struggling with Lyme Disease or any other chronic illness to find resources in your life; people or places, to help you turn within to your own deep heart. Your heart is wise and knowing. It bears much love, even for your wounded self, and it holds faithful energy, always beating for you, sustaining your lifeblood.

Take a moment to close your eyes, take some long deep breaths, put your hand over your heart and feel its steady presence. Thank this beautiful heart of yours for its power and patience, and in this moment say to your own self- "I love you", and really mean it.

We need to love ourselves in these times of distress. It is from the inside that we heal. Medicines, doctors, foods, others may minister to us from the outside, but we too must minister to our own selves on the inside. Healing takes time, it asks for restoration. The trauma of chronic illness wounds the heart and the spirit. Not everyone knows how to mend a broken spirit.

In the meantime, tending to your own precious heart energy and special self is an invaluable step in helping align your inner healing resources. I practiced this simple self-love for years and it has helped me recover from advanced Lyme Disease. It is worth trying and sticking with. I continue this practice still.

16

BELIEVE AND SEE

It is vital to use the power of your mind-body healing capacities. You must **BELIEVE** in your vibrant future. You must **SEE** yourself there. Belief is a powerful energy. It triggers the brain to create healthy, feel good neurotransmitters, which in turn jump starts the immune system. **BELIEF** is something we can each instill. **YOU** can set a healing intention of your own. You can set an image of yourself in your mind's eye that is strong and vital and glowing.

I believe in the power of the mind, the calling of our heart, and the mighty force of our will. When we can draw on these inner resources well, then we can move mountains. We can affect change. We can heal ourselves, others, the planet. If we can all focus together, aligning our hearts and minds in a common energy, then that unified force gains power and momentum.

Close your eyes if it helps you to center. Put your hand over your heart. In your mind's eye see yourself as powerful and strong. Now, drop your awareness from your mind, down into your heart. Feel its steady, knowing presence. Now we bind our mind, our heart and willpower with an intention.

I speak these words of healing intention, with hope. Hope for your healing, for the Lyme community's healing and for an end to this epidemic. Here are my words of healing intention:

I believe in a healthy future for myself, for my loved ones and those who suffer with Lyme disease.

I trust that the right people, resources and energies will align to arrest this epidemic.

With my own personal will and intention, I move forward into a happier, healthier, Lyme-free tomorrow.

May each and every one of us be guided and protected today and always.

17

DAY BY DAY

I watched evening descend. Soft skies, honeysuckle and birdsong filling my senses. A quiet periwinkle lingered to almost 9pm. Grace and beauty painted the perimeter of my sight. What a nightfall. I felt blessed.

Next, these words came to me — potent and vivid, as a guided tool to help those needing spiritual assistance. Whether health issues, emotional woes or financial burdens are weighing on you, take a moment to follow this visualization healing exercise. It will help ease off the energy that is draining and hampering you, and shift you within, to one of more true vibration.

Imagine your own spirit rising up from the crumpled, weary body or otherwise hampered condition it vies with. Sense your spirit when it is above you, how free and unencumbered the state is.

Write down the sensations, images, words that come to you.

Talk to your spirit-self. Remind 'it' how grateful you are for it holding on in spite of all this that you struggle with.

With your eyes closed ask your spirit what it most needs to change in your vibration in order to overcome illness, suffering or burdens.

Listen.

Grab that message. Write it down- anything that comes to you. Even if it's just one word. Keep it somewhere nearby to look at.

Every day take a moment to recall this awareness. Be with it. Embrace it. Read the words out loud to yourself. You will start the mind-body healing pathway.

This practice will help over time. Keep it up for months.

You are blessed.

Step by step, day by day, I meet the sun, the sky, the ebony night and the unknown challenges, plus the remarkable beauty of it all.

18

MAY WE BE GRACED

I am blessed. I am guided. I am protected. I am grateful. I am honored. I will bring my best work forward to the world. May we be graced in our relationships together.

19

THE VOID

The emptying, the void, no self, a place of quietude, stillness. Not a place often visited or well-tended in western society. We are not taught to cultivate our ability to empty and be in a void. This 'Inner Eden' is lush, fertile, ripe with beauty, receptivity, acceptance, endurance; the feminine. Yet, the process of getting there, the emptying, letting go of the needs, the ego, is difficult, frightening for many and 'against the grain' of most masculine- yang postures- of building status, prowess, defense and acquisition.

The state of the night- I love the night- embodies the feminine, reassuring darkness and the enveloping quiet. Mysterious, knowing, less action oriented, night times in the countryside are star-filled, twinkled with nature's sounds, dreams or deep crying, as a soul scans and reflects. Creative offspring are often seeded in the void.

Dawn brings the miracle of awakening. Light sheds, illuminating as all that is hidden. Vision is restored. Movement begins. Plants grow, animals and humans do more-forage, hunt, build, gather, procure. Nirvana though, found in the state of the 'dawning' is actually the awakening. This great miraculous gift of realization is in opposition to the space of austerity, emptiness, and the un-clarity in the darkness of The Void.

And we must move between both states fluidly daily, with our sun's rhythms, and in our life path as we close and expand periodically. We draw in, empty, get still and enter the void. Then, we open, awaken, become aware and grow. Nirvana is the wondrous joy of such physical and spiritual awakening. We must learn to respect, observe our self and move with the rhythms of our sleep and wake cycles in unison with the dark and light and our human growth of self-awareness.

20

MAY WE EMBRACE OUR PURPOSE

May we all be able to embrace our purpose, our heart's desire, to be open to destiny and meet with the God force moving through and around each of us; to bring healing and hope, peace and love to all we encounter.

21

BE FILLED WITH LIGHT

As the sun dipped to the horizon, golden light splayed across my shoulders and onto the lovely faces encircled together in the simple sanctuary. As I lit each person's candle and we each set an intention, I watched the eastern sky fade to lavender and tears float on eyelashes. Threaded together in harmonious convergence, beauty and grace washed us. Thirty precious souls stepped forward to change lives and futures in the Lyme disease battle, and to herald a dawning of a new age in healing.

I felt the power of our union in that quaint sanctuary in Canada, among brave warriors. My mission continues. May all of us thrive, and may our lives be filled with light and love and health.

22

WORKING FROM OUR
HIGHEST GOOD

Enlightenment is not gained overnight or at a two-week retreat or a month in an ashram (all lovely experiences), but it comes through a death spiral of fear and grief and the most courageous fortitude and trial of endurance you could ever fathom. Enlightenment is more grueling than childbirth or an Ironman triathlon or surviving a house fire. The rebirth after our spiritual death is filled with a dewy tender breath of beauty and gifts of unsuspect possibility. Enlightenment brings serenity and deep wisdom and a calm internal pool of simplicity. Enlightenment is eternal. Once there, one never turns back to the old life.

My journey to death's door made me surrender to what I grasped onto and felt was my identity and power and props. I know so much more now. And, still I learn every single day.

I attune to the process of accepting that I am unfolding once again. Letting go, receiving and growing with the seasons, the rhythms, the magic of life and the precious process of being a vessel of love and light, whether in times of darkness or moments of maximum joy.

May all of us be protected and guided and work from our highest good. I embrace the future. What is calling to you?

23

OPTIMAL HEALTH IN A STORMY CROSSING

Even as a holistic health care practitioner myself, I had to examine my life and what made me fall so ill and vulnerable to these microbes, and to allow myself the time and process to embrace transformation at all planes—physically, emotionally, mentally, and spiritually. As a homeopath, I thought I was versed in helping others heal. This experience asked me to learn even more.

When we fall ill to chronic disease we fracture in a certain way. Things are never quite the same. There is a sense of displacement or that you just do not feel quite right and that you want to correct it all. What I suggest is that something rather grand is being asked of you in this time of disorder. You are being asked to reflect upon your life status—your behaviors and choices and your habits. And then, you are being asked to make some changes in order to mend.

Why do some of us fall ill to these conditions but not others? And, most importantly, how can I mend from the disease or divorce or depression and reclaim my well-being and vitality?

The great arc presiding over the entire journey for me, however, has been the enormous breadth and depth of spirituality's presence. Difficult states, like serious diseases present, ultimately bring us into concert with energy beyond the simple self. We are entering the domain of personal transformation and what in modern times is akin to a quest—a quest for higher knowledge, for inner strength, and for assistance in the darkest of times. This journey asks for faith and guidance and an unfurling of the powerful connection we innately bear between our mind and our body and our spirit. For we are marvelous and miraculous beings. We just need to learn how to stitch it all together.

We bear enormous internal gifts. However, many of us have not been taught how to "turn on" the healing codes, or we have forgotten. Mending helps us find our inner compass, to re-calibrate during a time of lost navigation and to set our sights on a positive outcome. Like any worthy voyage, not every day is a smooth passage. But you can still reach your destination! Optimal health and happiness can be attainable even in a stormy crossing.

We will chart a course together through the pivotal domain of personal transformation. For true healing happens on the inside.

24

11:11

11:11 is my reminder that the risks I have been taking to be a pioneer, to live selflessly, to let go of my old 'comfort' zone and to help awaken others is just what I am supposed to be doing and in all honesty, I love it, though some nights I fall into bed bone tired from the endless energy I pour out into others and into the world, sometimes in group or mass settings. It is wonderful, enlightening, expansive and something I can NOT stop paying attention to. Healing energy moves through me in such creative ways. I marvel at the flow of it all.

25

COURAGE TO BE WHOLE

My heart and spirit are with you all. Please know I care deeply about bringing healing and strength to our culture. As we go through the changes and transformations at hand, we can all come out the other side more brilliant and aware than ever.

Believe in yourself, in your truth, in our unique gifts, and your courage to be happy and whole again.

26

TRUTH

Truth is an awareness. A place of complete acceptance. No facades, barriers, gates, or mechanizations. Pure and crystalline, truth shows complete acceptance by being in inner repose—a calmness, a serene knowing. Emotions and mental thought processes do not clutter truth.

Truth asks for clarity within. An open channel to source. Truth asks for composure, listening, and most profoundly, a core belief that all is well.

27

LIFE WITH A MISSION

My message has been to use my own ten-year recovery story and decades of natural medicine restoration knowledge to enlighten, inspire and bring education to so many weary and suffering souls in need of direction and living proof that healing and full vibrant life restoration is possible.

Having looked death straight in the eye and brazenly said "NO" – "I am going to live", I have been given a second chance at life and I walk it with honor and dignity. My grassroots campaign, united with Lyme disease support groups worldwide, my two books, my creative brainchild – 'Lyme Light Radio' and deeply held passion to bring spiritual and emotional healing with my energetic mind-body healing skills comes purely from a higher calling within me.

I am a humanitarian. This path I walk is more about you and the masses I wish to 'touch' than about me. Ego dissolves when you defy death and come back to life with a mission.

28

HEALING HAPPENS ON THE INSIDE

I have met thousands and thousands of people in these last five years out on the road. I have treated thousands in my private practice over these 35 years. I have interviewed some of the world's most talented specialists and researchers. I taught with some of the greatest health care practitioners of our time. I have learned so very much. And, deep within my core, I sense the weary, the wounded, the searching souls whom are tired of suffering, with scant support of recovery.

You are not alone. I am here because I care. There are many of us here because we care. The absolutely sterling, fine people I have met, whom host me while on book tours, at support group visits across this nation, in foreign countries and whom join me in facing this Lyme disease crisis are brave and resourceful and strong. You are too! Belief is a life altering tool we carry within. It is one of the seven inner gifts we bear for igniting the mind-body healing pathway. Seven is a magical number. You own your personal inner magic.

Healing happens on the inside. Let's shift the plates in your life path. I believe in you.

29

DEEP REST

Like the revolving seasons of nature, we must honor times of deep rest, those of creative juices and the hard work of harvesting our efforts.

30

PASSAGEWAY THROUGH CHANGE

I recall the exact day my world changed in what I consider to be traumatic proportions. A day seared in my memory forever, for its tender breaths of love, and also for its portents of devastation. My young son and I picnicked in our sun splashed backyard, playing catch and collecting stray balls from the deep fern glade. I still hold this day with a certain reverence, for it marks the beginning of the end of the world I once loved. A world I worked very hard to create.

However, nothing lasts forever. Little did I know winds of change were in the air. In the end, every shred of my cherished existence would be ripped away, leaving me shattered, shaking and forlorn, deep on the ocean floor of life. It would become a trial in loss, fortitude and profound lessons. And, most amazingly, it would also become a passageway through transformative changes and rebirth that I could never have willingly conjured.

Lyme disease stripped me of everything: my career, income, home, marriage and health. My journey to the underworld of life was akin to Persephone. The months and years of isolation, floating bereft on my sofa detached from the world and its social happenings, lost from my children's school activities, instead forced me into personal retreat from life and brought me into a very mystical place of stillness. My inner journey of healing was as profound as all the physical ministering we tended to.

As human beings we are remarkably elastic, evolving and adaptive. We can re-frame our thoughts and cells and our vibration, as well as our health status in so many different facets. Lyme disease forced me to change, to dig deep, to reflect and grow into a person of greater wisdom and clarity and now infused with passion and mission to end the suffering too many of thousands, like myself, endure. Renewed and well, I live with deep respect and gratitude for the many miracles each day presents and the beautiful synergy of compassion I meet in the faces of everyday life. I feel honored and am blessed to have a second chance at life. May the sun and stars and gifts of rebirth guide and protect my journey and yours.

31

SPIRIT CALLING FOR CHANGE

Serious illness is our spirit's calling for ultimate full-life change. All our bodily systems, energy chakra and emotional fabric are being asked to transform. You can no longer run on your old "grid." That pattern was not as healthy and productive as you may have perceived it to be, even if aspects of your life felt rewarding or fulfilling. I was a homeopath with a thriving practice in a quaint New England village. I sat on the national board and wrote the national exam. I was a wife, a mom, a great neighbor and caring friend. I thought I was doing everything right and Lyme disease took me down- way deep down- and asked me, forced me, to change. This illness is powerful and asks you to summon your own powers.

Our life steward- the wise guide- our connection to the divine reaches us no matter what our circumstances, no matter how fixed we are in our lifestyle or defense postures. When it is time to change, our life steward presents the opportunity- it is more deeply understood as personal transformation. Personal transformation is a deep, soulful journey, akin to Persephone's descent into the underworld and hell-fires of personal demons and treacherous obstacles, even what some call imprisonment. But, ultimately, if we listen within, and we learn how to let go and with the ability to find faith, trust, balance and self-love, we can re-calibrate, receive divine guidance, and grow in vastness and depth. We return to the land of light and the living refreshed and graced with creative outpourings and ultimately an open channel to the Divine.

Like a mother who is willing to sacrifice her own self needs to another's well-being, we too must accept the gesture of self-nurturance. This is not an easy task at first for most of us in modern western society. We put others ahead of ourselves, including job demands, chores, partners and our children. This is all acceptable, to a point. But where is the balance point? That fulcrum of sacrifice and self-care? Serious illness or life crisis puts a BRIGHT spotlight on this very intrinsic life sustaining issue.

Everyone, myself included, afflicted with chronic disease, must delve into their personal relationship with Self. What can be let go of? What do you now sacrifice in order to heal? Lyme disease, various illnesses and mental imbalances have cycles and our body recognizes these phases via symptom states. And, personally, we all have our own rhythms. These rhythms must be honored. Our culture is forgetting how to; all we do is push harder and faster.

When we are seriously ill, the hamster wheel absolutely must stop; Immediately! No more multitasking, charging, late hours, ignoring your time for quiet and serenity. In fact, most chronic illness cases ask a being to enter the domain of retreat and solitude, to move inwards and open to divinity's tapping's.

You are being called. Can you hear the whisper, feel the urge, the desire? If not, I will help you. We will find that pearl of Spirit calling. It is in your heart-space, waiting for you to claim it. You can claim this precious gem, and in turn nourish your self-intimacy, for then, when we look to create balance- not fight the tide or push upstream- but instead accept the ebbs and flows, like moon cycles and nature's seasons, does our psyche, our spirit and eventually our cells and body find balance or homeostasis and return to wellness. This journey is sacrificial. Like the shedding of autumn foliage, we must let go!

Drugs, herbs, supplements, diets, are critical external tools offering support for better systemic function. These are our helpmates on the material plane. But on the internal plane, at the metaphysical juncture only you- hear me, only YOU- can make these shifts. Only you can create shifts of consciousness, only you can open to your higher source, only you, only you can learn to honor your rhythms, love yourself, attune to nature and in fact, it is you that can set deep healing in motion.

We are not compartmentalized beings, comprised just of body parts, but we are integrated and whole, fascinating, creative, resilient creatures with facile minds and ever-evolving feelings and powers. It is my role to serve as your guide into the domain of spiritual healing and accessing the mind-body pathway.

32

YOUR MOST POWERFUL ALLY

Your spirit is mighty, your heart is filled with love and your mind is one of your most powerful allies.

33

TENDING A BROKEN SPIRIT

Tending to a broken spirit is just as essential as mending a broken body.

34

DEEP JOURNEY

Personal transformation is a deep, soulful journey, akin to Persephone's descent into the underworld. Ultimately, if we listen within, and we learn how to let go and with the ability to find faith, trust, balance and self-love, we can recalibrate, receive divine guidance, and grow in vastness and depth.

35

ALL IS POSSIBLE

I am here because I have been in your shoes and I made that frightening, death-call journey into Hades and back out here into the light. I am here to remind you with my presence and renewed health and vitality that anything is possible! Your spirit is mighty, your heart is filled with love and your mind one of your most powerful allies. Your future is yours to create. ALL is possible.

36

THRIVING VERSUS SURVIVING

Coping helps us endure and survive. It embodies fortitude. But coping has a limit, too. Coping is not a freeing state or an enthused state. It is a state of management. This is Ok, and actually commendable. But I remind you that something more is being asked of you than coping. What I bring to you is the image of hope and the tool of inspiration, for this tandem of beliefs can jumpstart your life path into one of endless opportunity and onto a journey of personal accomplishments beyond the effects of any outside individual or medicine or physician.

When do we let go of merely coping and embrace true healing and the evolution of growth and well-being, which ultimately can become so rewarding and filled with fresh light that we expand beyond our self and the ego, and our held patterns? We then strive and thrive in ways beyond even our own expectations, and venture beyond the container of our individual self and contribute to the world in some significant way, then we begin to do something more than the ordinary; we do the extraordinary; we THRIVE!

'Thrivers' lend their self to the world way beyond the ego level, to contribute to mankind. Thrivers have experienced hellacious decimation and when they look death in the eye, in its all too many forms, thrivers change their interior grid. They let go of the temporal and their coping forms and transform to a new form of their own self, that brings something extraordinary to life. They bring their highest, best good to the world. And, the *thriver* exists in all of us-- it is a matter of allowing yourself to let go, make that pivot turn, and to tap into your personal gift or life contribution.

37

THUNDERSTORM OF CHANGE

One droplet of rain does not feel like very much. But, a million droplets create a thunderstorm. By binding together, we can invoke a thunderstorm of change.

38

THE LESSON OF CHARACTER

Developing character is one of life's true lessons. Chronic illness stripped me down to bare bones and I re-bloomed with greater wisdom and a calling to end the Lyme disease epidemic.

39

RESILIENCY

Resiliency is the distinguishing quality that helps people rebound and often grow with wisdom as they recoup from the hard knocks of life. In the world of natural medicine, we recognize resilient individuals as having a lot of vitality and deep willpower. Some people seem to have an innate resiliency, but it can also be cultivated.

40

YOUR SPIRIT IS MIGHTY

Your spirit is mighty and giving yourself time to move through the phases of trauma and recovery, without getting caught in fear or self-pity or self-neglect can make for a resilient swing back.

41

BLESSED TO BE

I have survived the Lyme disease calamity—I work daily to voice the need for recognition, Integrative Medicine, spiritual healing for the very weary and worn. I am blessed to be a messenger and healing vessel for many.

42

COMFORT AND INSPIRATION

As human beings we need nurturing and care when we are ill. I wrote "Out of the Woods" as a handhold of comfort and inspiration, to the all too many who suffer with this illness. The Lyme epidemic has flown under the radar for decades, leaving an estimated 3,000,000 people stricken in various stages of this chronic form, often misdiagnosed as an autoimmune illness. "Out of the Woods" offers diagnostic and treatment guidance. Most vividly, it puts voice to the emotional experience the Lyme collective shares. I offer it as a talisman of hope, and a light of inspiration that you too can heal.

43

DISPEL THE BLOCKS

When we have 'blocks' or holding patterns established by unresolved or contained emotions, often affiliated with an illness, trauma or suppressed stories, we inhibit our body's natural energetic flow. If we hold these patterns for any length of time, the physical body, its organs and glands, can become impaired, sending us distress signals; pain and malfunction being very common. We want to dispel these blocks and restore fluidity.

44

TAPPING LIFE FORCE

By honoring your inner light, by being conscious about it and surrounding yourself with positive people, beauty, the colors you love, youthful children and individuals, and the wonderment of each daily personal encounter with people and nature, and the magic of synchronicity, you are tapping into a spiritual state of renewal and life force. This is the power of your own being in an alignment to higher source, or divinity, to what many refer to as God or the Universe. But ultimately you must acknowledge a recognition within, that you are able and capable of using your own belief and mindset and personal inner Self to make change.

45

THE LABYRINTH

Every New Year's our quaint hamlet hosts an extraordinary event; we walk a Labyrinth, the same formation as the sacred one at Chartres Cathedral in France. The one that priests and mystics, common folk and royalty have moved through with intention, in prayer or trance for centuries.

We are blessed to have devoted community members in our town 'tape' the entire geometric pattern out in exact mathematical proportions faithfully and with precision each December 31 and hold it until 5:00 pm on January 1. Many of us volunteer as 'guardians', taking one-hour shifts, overseeing the safe-keeping, offering guidance, keeping candles lit, holding a space of reverence, while people of the community move into a New Year with Intention. It is very touching.

In stockinged feet, the snows banking the sturdy brick hall, the old floorboards creak under the thousands of paces taken, as youngsters scamper and the elderly shuffle though the lovely labyrinth. Our old 'hippie stock', the local business folks, ministers, dancers, college kids home for the holidays and out of town family mingle, passing in strides, sitting cross-legged in the clover leaf styled center for contemplation.

I love that our town holds this tradition, that we honor an ancient spiritual practice, that we blend and move in silence for 24 hours. Sometimes a pianist or fiddler brings us live accompaniment, often we play chant music in backdrop. I am one of the guardians. It is always a privilege to be part of the graceful syncopations and transcendent energy being created on the dawn of a New Year.

This year's Labyrinth was as beautiful as always, winter's low cast light streaming in amber rays through the windows, participants bowed heads, conveying thoughtfulness, openness to divinity and of course, many in prayer. Whenever I bring an outsider to our annual Labyrinth, they leave in awe - the chaotic outside world evaporates, beauty and symmetry are so potent, peace and simplicity overarching tones. There is grace. Spirit is summoned in a common Town Hall.

Many gestures of communion, friendship, love always ensues for me each year - a Labyrinth breeds harmonious undertones. Inside the sacred space we do not talk, but out in the foyer whispered conversations burble.

This year a woman rushed up to me, earnest eyes, hands outstretched, blonde hair capped in woven wool. "Katina, it is because of you that my life is restored. You saved me!" I did not recognize her. Yet, her smile, our handholding was so real.

"I went to your Lyme talk a year and a half ago at the Grange and you educated us about the faulty Western Blot Test readings by the average GP's. I remembered that. This summer I was deathly ill and my doctor said that 'one band' positive on the Lyme disease test did not confirm Lyme. He said I didn't have the illness. I kept getting sicker".

"Thank you for replying to me email and referring me to Dr.X, she immediately put me on 2 months of antibiotics, followed by herbs for Lyme and I recovered!" joy streaming from her cornflower blue eyes.

"That is wonderful. I'm so happy to learn I helped you, and that you jumped on the treatments."

"You saved my life Katina, and your educational work and healing mission is so important. In fact, you are changing consciousness. Please keep writing and speaking and hosting the 'Lyme Light Radio' show."

I felt deeply touched there in the New England white clapboard, mahogany railed foyer. Though others acknowledge my mission often, something in that moment of critical honesty made me realize the thousands of miles I have travelled in 7 years, the hundreds of thousands of words I have written on this subject, the endless hours of conversation and healing sessions I have ministered are not in vain.

I had entered my "walk of intention" into the Labyrinth maze on New Year's Day, with a focus to bring *my books* and my Inspirational speaking into International circulation, with the purpose of uniting the powers of Spirit and doctoring in harmony. My Intention is to help the weary reclaim their inner healing skills, tools I know how to teach. I want health, comfort, support for us all.

This moment of meeting, while parting from our sacred Labyrinth, reminded me to keep 'walking the maze' of life. Like the priests and nuns and seekers of yore, a heart open to guidance and a mind available to creativity, will stay attuned and in turn the purposeful progress of moving with intention will manifest and my pathway will be illuminated. Each of our unique paths, in fact, will show the way.

May we all be able to embrace our purpose, our heart's desire, to be open to destiny and meet with the God force moving through and around each of us; to bring healing and hope, peace and love to all we encounter.

A new year dawns with a clarity for me within, yet a chock-full life of demands from the outside. May I maintain my balance point, may my muse remain fed, may my loved ones be blessed and may the higher calling I am moved by, as brilliantly vivid as the guiding North star, hold me fast.

46

YOU ARE MIRACULOUS

Move out and forward into your future and do it with your own natural beauty and empowered with your belief in your most sterling you. For you are wise and strong and miraculous. You can overcome obstacles and burdens and shadows. You can embrace change and let the light inside of you shine.

47

TO BE SUMMONED

Most chronic illness cases ask a being to enter the domain of retreat and solitude, to move inwards and open to divinity's tapping's.

You are being summoned. Can you hear the whisper, feel the urge, the desire?

The time has come to honor your spirit, not the expectations your upbringing imprinted you with or the template of overwork and no time for play and relaxation that society has catapulted you into over recent decades.

Take this timeout from life's pace and demands to JUST be with your spirit.

48

SEE BEYOND THE SUF-FERING

Fear, insecurity, anger, shock, sadness can be overwhelming. But we were each blessed with a mind, and willpower and a heart of true love and courage. When sick we need to turn on these precious inner tools. People who thrive in spite of disaster; shipwreck survivors, war torn victims, refugees, and even Lyme disease *recoverees* all share something in common. Even in the throes of the horror, they SEE themselves in a better future. They see themselves happy, whole and healthy. They SEE beyond their suffering into a better place.

49

POWER OF WILL

Lyme disease is a journey of spiritual transformation. It makes us dig deep, it makes us fight with the strongest fortitude of a warrior, it makes us reach beyond the limits of our self, of our ego, of the parameters of what you have been taught is medicine and healing and find the great gifts of your own powerful inner resources; the power of will, intention, and purpose.

50

YOUR TEST

For ultimately, this journey-no matter how horrid and frightening and maddening it feels at times-- is real-- and it is your journey—akin to the old pilgrimage walks and Holy Grail quests of ancient times. You are being tested- and you can summit the peak and find your way through this crossing to a place of wellness and vitality and rebirth.

51

HERE ON PURPOSE

I am here on purpose - I am here FOR YOU and BECAUSE OF YOU- to plant a seedling of vision and intention into your mind's eye and will force. Like the phoenix who rose from the ashes, I rose above the deep death call of advanced deadly disease, to beat the odds. I am here because I have been guided from forces greater than me - to exemplify that you too can rise again like a phoenix and rebuild a new life, a new path and to birth something of your creativity and purpose. You can move beyond illness, despair, dissatisfaction and fear to a place of fulfilment.

52

FREEDOM TO EXPAND

or the deepest message I received from those dark
cavernous days and nights of illness and loss, is that
something is crying to be born from you-- a life passion or
heart's desire or even the act of letting go of your past patterns
and setting a new energy grid. You can move above and beyond
the deep, dark, depressing, negative low energy state of the ugly
borrelia burgdorferi and rise to a higher vibration that no longer
permits room for this organism to flourish in and allows you
the freedom to expand into the most beautiful and authentic
being you want to be.

53

ACCEPT CHANGE

Any life catastrophe; a worn-out marriage, a serious illness, addictions, bankruptcy, a family crisis are a form of a death call-- literally and metaphysically- and it is an incredible opportunity to take a dire life challenge and work with it. To accept change, to honor your life's hidden yearnings and to no longer fight the tides, the people who don't really see you for whom you are. These experiences are a critical call from your spirit to commit to your truest path. Healing your SELF is within your grasp and also something beyond you is calling, reaching out, asking for you to move beyond the Self and into mankind.

54

THE QUEST

Ultimately the quest to healing is a journey of personal transformation. It is not for the faint of heart. If you are ill or suffering in any form, you are being tested and tried, and are being asked to exhibit your most profound fortitude, to face the trickery of mental trappings and the dark demons of emotional pitfalls. The turn we take inwards is when the true healing begins. For though externally directed doctoring may address infections and massive depletions and damages, the real magic of healing happens on the inside when we can turn on our mind and our spirit in unison with our heart and really LISTEN within, to our intuition.

55

HARNESS YOUR BELIEF

God speaks to us each in unique ways. My temples are the forests of nature, others find a house of worship and some of you discover your connection to divinity in the quiet still hours of prayer. But turning on BELIEF is a megawatt healing tool, and you know what? Belief is something we all contain. It is for free and it is yours to harness and actually build in abundance.

56

PHOENIX RISING

Most importantly, you must dig deep!! You must find your inner strength and willpower, you must remember that you are a very wise being whom has been somehow neglecting your special gift and life calling for assorted reasons, like over-working, multitasking, valuing other things or even loved ones more than your very own precious self. But Lyme and autoimmune disease will not let that pattern continue any longer. Life crisis asks us to reach inside to our very core, to get very still, to re-calibrate and to honor our knowing. For you are wise and you are powerful, and you CAN mend and be re-birthed. YOU TOO ARE A PHOENIX. We all are.

57

TODAY I AM STRONGER

Today I am stronger than my yesterdays. Tomorrow I move into the future. Being here in this moment is my process of living, learning, discovering. I hold true to my wonderfully creative and vibrant spirit, and live each day with pride and passion, knowing that life is a precious journey of sharing and caring, opportunity and most miraculously, gilded with guidance from a higher power. I am open to the teachings being given to me and agree to share with others. I live with gratitude, and in pure respect of the powers of healing.

58

THE SOOTHSAYER

The International Lyme and Associated Disease Society conference held in sunny San Diego was a sight to behold. 420 attendees from all over the globe, on lush Paradise Point Resort. I must say it was a true privilege to be conversing and dining with world class researchers, doctors, practitioners, advocates, innovative thinkers, risk taking individuals and many Lyme patients. My mind was swarming with new information, brilliant moments of synchronicity and the backdrop of glimmering Mission Bay bathing us all in good fortune and promise for creating a healthier Lyme-free or at least Lyme-controlled tomorrow.

As we dined al fresco, Perseus Major, Venus and the golden full moon bathing us in a fluid blend of companionship, passionate commitment to a public health crisis, and the poetry of inner attunement to mankind's plight, I felt at times as if I was living in a chrysalis of another reality. Like we were gestating and weaving together; harmonies, individual talents, trainings, visions and the personal 'Lyme trench' experience of tragedy, coming to the table in a certain gestalt, preparing for the birth of something very important.

At ILADS, I listened to the brilliant and interesting presentations on co-infections, glutathione pathways, retroviruses, biofilms, endocrine disorders, Hyperbaric oxygen therapy and much more. The very obvious pattern at this year's ILADS was that it was VERY treatment based and less science research focused compared to 2013. Practitioners left with many ideas and tools to implement with their cases, helping to rebuild depletions, attack infections, and to a veteran Homeopath like me, the most ASTOUNDING realization was that **Integrative Medicine was being promoted**!

Thirty years ago, as a newbie Classical Homeopath I was looked at as an oddball at a cocktail party, my job too 'weird' sounding for many to stomach. To find this cutting edge, open minded Medical based health care community gladly reaching to enzyme therapy, homeopathic formulas, detoxification methods and herbs to kill bugs and rebuild damage was beyond my wildest imaginings from decades ago (antibiotics still in full force for acute infections and dire central nervous system issues). BUT, if it takes a public health care crisis, called Lyme disease, to marry the two hands of health care, well then let it be!

To quote Thomas Edison: *"The doctor of the future will give no medication but will interest his patients in the care of the human frame, diet and in the cause and prevention of disease. ~ "*

Lyme Disease can be a deadly illness. It affects every person in a unique way beyond the initial feverish, flu-like pains and malaise of the acute phase. It morphs and lingers, disseminates and moves its way into the central nervous system- ALS, Parkinson's, Bells Palsy, Lupus, CFS, migraines all too ugly when not 'caught' quickly enough. Hourly, I learned a death story by Lyme disease from an attendee. This illness can NO longer be brushed off. We must work HARD! We need billions of dollars, the way AIDS received in the 1990's, to crack the code.

A particularly poignant moment came for me, when a small group of four of us stood on the soft San Diego beach sand, city lights littering the bay and a giant full moon dangling overhead, nurturing and inspiring the Earth. Renowned physician Dr. Kenneth Liegner serenaded us with his marvelous trumpet playing, ending with a very moving rendition of TAPS, played in memorial for all those who have died due to Lyme disease. Our hearts hung heavy and I was deeply touched to be in such sterling company of dedicated people.

It was my great privilege to give the inspirational address at the San Diego Lyme Walk and Rally. What a great group was there! How many impassioned voices, hardworking folks and frail victims.

I have survived the Lyme Calamity. I work daily to voice the need for recognition, Integrative Medicine, spiritual healing for the very weary and worn. *"Lyme Light Radio with Katina"* is a channel of dialogue, education, tools to battle this problem.

I left ILADS buoyed with hope. Brilliant, devoted people converged for four days, learning, sharing, caring about this illness, the victims, what they can bring to the table, what they can bring home and utilize. Or how they can better educate or evoke change of consciousness.

Meanwhile, I packed up Sunday night and had a delicious water-side dinner with old friends. While walking along the bay, a wizened old Haitian witchdoctor sat crossed legged on the grass alongside the quay in the park, reading palms and telling futures. Ever curious me, I sat down with the aged one, leathered dark skin, glowing amber eyes, peering deeply into my own. I asked for a 'reading'.

"I am in the presence of an angel" he spoke and bowed to me, taking my hands, cupping them in his warmth. "You are a gifted and powerful healer, a soul older than my own. My skin prickles with your mighty powers bathing me now," his lyrical voice streamed.

I felt my spine tingle and was caught a bit off-guard and even doubting. The soft California night whispered in the palm trees. He sprinkled me with "Florida Water" and said, "You will not pay me for this time. It is not right. You are a mystic. It is my privilege to be with you now."

I did not know what to think. But I listened.

"A man has left your side recently (my mate, Hunter, this June). A family member, a powerful man, died three years ago (my dad). But, do not worry, I very big heart will be with you soon. Someone grand and generous who understands you are a very rare person is coming in the future. A man of deep love and wealth. You will have five grandchildren. You are on a mission, like a saint or Queen. Do not hesitate or feel sad for yourself ever. Your eyes tell me it all. You have seen the great mysteries of the Universe. I can teach you even more, the old ways of African priests. You will heal thousands, maybe millions. Allow me to teach you."

I am sitting, listening, semi-uncertain and beckon my best friend of 43 years over to hear this. She sits near me. She listens, too. She smiles at the witchdoctor when he repeats, "She is an angel." She nods a *yes*.

He proceeds. More prophecies are shared, some about my writing work and speaking to large masses of people. I do not know what to truly absorb. Eventually, with the cool night steeped in purple hues, I stand and bow to the old man. He hands me his bracelet, a worn woven wrap and a CD of his own healing music.

"I pass this to you. Protection in the sea of life. I will pray for you every day. Come here again. I will teach you to SEE even deeper. Through thousands of years."

"I live 3500 miles away, it is impossible," comes my reply.

"Nothing is impossible. You are a master healer. I will teach you, even if I must come to where you are. I have been waiting for you to appear from my dream for a very long time. I must do a ceremonial cleansing Botanica on you for more teaching to come. Are you here tomorrow to take the rites?"

"No, I fly out in the morning."

Is this guy a nut or truly a sage? Now, completely bewitched with eve falling, I shake hands with the crinkled one.

"Thank you for seeing my true essence," come my words of gratitude. "You are a kind man, and very generous."

"I am only reminding you to BE who you are," his Haitian accent, jumbled and colored with rhythms and melody convey. "Very big work lies ahead for you. Do not be afraid. Your spirit knows what to do. Just listen to it. I will not push you. But you will call me when you are ready to learn more. As a mystic you know just what I mean- words are not necessary." He smiles, yellowed teeth flashing in a quick crescent. "God bless you, Angel of Compassion. You move with God's protection."

We walk away, or rather I float away. I am anointed in ancient magic, while simultaneously steeped in four days of modern medical training. What do I think? How am I the conduit, the elixir, the carrier of Mother Earth's Universal wisdom entwined with Western medicine's scientific workings. My senses swim. I am in semi-trance, all of this somehow stewed together within an eclipsing health crisis and a full golden moon riding in the Eastern sky?

Nancy looks at me, grinning her mischievous smile.

"Leave it to you, to find a witch-doctor in the wake of this weekend of left brained didactics. Somehow, you manage to meld the two halves of healing, old and new, heaven and earth."

We both chuckled, our eyes locked together in a smile; over four decades under our belt as soul-sisters, with my mysterious nature always magnetically drawing unusual folks and circumstances out of the blue.

"I don't know what to really think of him?" I question her.

Pragmatic, poised, regal Nancy soothes, "He is correct. You are a powerful healer, he probably really does want to help you and YES, you are positioned exactly in the midst of a health care crisis with personal experience and professional knowledge and skills unique to all others. I believe his vision that you are destined for something important. It is just for us to wonder if he is a charlatan or not regarding the training? Sit on it for a few days, you will know."

I nod. I ponder. I sense. I want to try his ancient African healing magic. And, I will leave on a jet plane in the morning. Somehow, I try to let it all sift through me. I feel a bit off kilter. But really, I intuit, I am just rebalancing. 'Prince Alex' the soothsayer helped recalibrate me in that reading. After days of science mind and analytical reasoning, he brought me into my right brain hemisphere of sensing, intuitive knowing.

Whether he is correct in his prophecies or not, it is OK. I must walk my path, lamplight of inspiration lit for those struggling. As a messenger I offer hope and faith and information. I 'move with God's protection', though the footpath is never so clear.

Step by step, day by day, I meet the sun, the sky, the ebony night and the unknown challenges, plus the remarkable beauty of it all. I am forever grateful for all who I meet in this incredible journey of discovery and living. Thank you ILADS for an absolutely stunning conference and groundbreaking work being shared. It was such an enormous privilege to be gathered with such talented people. The sun, the moon and the stars all aligned for the highest good.

59

IN PARTING

I hope my messages have given you some new perspectives and motivation to really allow your purest form of you to bloom. My next book, *"Mind Body Spirit Medicine with Katina; Finding Sanctuary"* is a companion to this and will include guidance and practical exercises on how to ignite your mind body spirit pathway, as well as how to tap into your innate wellspring of very potent powers we house, but may need to cultivate.

Thank you for your kinship - readers, friends, the sick, the lonely, the seekers and healers. Our lives are not by accident. This earth time is precious and ever evolving. I walk it with you, at pace, and in peace, to a beautiful, healthier tomorrow. I do not regret for one moment to decision to follow the eagle guide on the threshold of my death and forge my way back to a life of full living and completely rebirthed. I would never have likely become a spiritual healer and learned how much power we all bear on the inside and from the unseen. The soothsayer summed it all up so succinctly… I have seen the mysteries of the ages and am here to guide and heal. Life is clearly not at all random.

Blessings to all.

Katina Makris, CCH, CIH
New Hampshire, USA
2019

ABOUT THE AUTHOR

Katina Makris, CCH, CIH has worked in natural health care since 1985, as a successful Certified Classical Homeopath and a popular newspaper health columnist. She sat on the board of The Council for Homeopathic Certification for seven years. She is also a Certified Intuitive Healer, focusing her current work on healing the spirit as well as the body.

Katina is the author of "Out of the Woods: Healing Lyme Disease - Body, Mind and Spirit" and "Autoimmune Illness and Lyme Disease Recovery Guide: Mending the Body, Mind, and Spirit". Both books promote Lyme disease awareness and inspirational guidance on Integrative Medicine treatment and recovery as well as metaphysics. Katina is valued for her wealth of experience and dynamic communication skills, as an international workshop leader, keynote speaker and host of the hit program "Lyme Light Radio with Katina". She is a tireless advocate, having presented 195 live speaking events in less than seven years.

Her decades of writing and teaching to the public has created an author and teacher with a warm, honest and engaging style. Katina's work is appreciated for its vivid emotional quotient as well as her ability to transcend the mundane into the core of what life and living, health and wellness, are really about. She touches the heart with her remarkable own personal transformation journey from bedridden to renewed and whole.

She has been both practitioner and patient. Katina's Mind Body Spirit Medicine teachings are changing lives for countless people.

Katina is a graduate of Duke University, The Stillpoint School of Integrative Life Healing, Hahnemann School of Homeopathy. USA New Book Finalist 2011. Top 50 Authors You Should Be Reading Award 2012.

Connect with Katina

Website: https://katinamakris.com
LinkedIn: https://www.linkedin.com/in/katina-makris-a0046725
Facebook: https://www.facebook.com/OutOfTheWoodsBook
Twitter: https://twitter.com/lymelightradio
Instagram: https://www.instagram.com/katinamakris

Katina invites you to join her at her online healing academy, to include an array of webinars and certification programs on a variety of natural medicine topics, mind body spirit practicums, Lyme and Autoimmune Disease recovery modules, organic living in the modern era, Inspirational teachings and more of her 38 years of high quality professional expertise.

ACKNOWLEDGEMENTS

This book has been written with love and delivered with compassion.

I would like to thank my publicist and manager, Robbi Gunter for prompting me to take my near-death transformational experience and personal writings and bring them forth as visions of hope and guidance for people seeking solace in a modern time of trials and dissatisfaction.

Thank you, Cecile Gough, Lyme disease warrior, former Oncology nurse and workshop colleague, for allowing me to bounce so many ideas off you in this writing process and for your keen eye for detail in finessing the final push to completion. Also, your graphic design work for my digital inspiration quotes are incredible.

To Jeanne Lise Pacy, your friendship and midnight talks as I shifted through my own levels of consciousness and doubts about creating this book have been truly invaluable. Your wisdom and frank ability to see what the future needs, motivated me to keep at this when I felt off kilter. Bless you.

Dearest longtime friend and colleague, Dr. Lonny Brown, thank you always for your healing work on me and your gifts of understanding, helping me through troubled waters. The final proofing and your generous endorsement of my work in the world touches me and our fire side chats keep me sane, when the outer world demands crash in!

Thank you, world acclaimed portrait and fashion photographer, Denis Batuev for our amazing photo shoots and synergy in capturing our cover photo and my lovely author portrait. You are such a master.

To my mentor, Dr. Meredith Young Sowers, though we were not communicating while I was compiling this work, I am forever indebted to you, as without you training me to become a certified Intuitive Spiritual healer over a decade ago, I would not have been as skillfully able to articulate the relationship between mind, body and spirit, that so profoundly has affected my life path and work.

As always, I must acknowledge the powerful gene pool of my eastern Mediterranean Greek ancestry. A clan of hard workers, true thrivers amid dire life adversities, and frank mystics dotted amongst my relatives, I am grateful for the messages and imprinting I received from you (many long deceased) mighty souls. You taught me resiliency, you mirrored ingenuity and fearlessness, and you all communed with the unseen realm with such ease. From you and my Quaker schooling, I learned at a very young age that each and every one of us is a resourceful and adaptive being, able to engage willpower, belief, faith and love in all forms.

And, lastly to my remarkable son Jake C. Hollander, thank you for your deep intuition. When I question my creative contributions to the world, your wise perceptions endlessly remind me to listen within.

Namaste my dear loved ones.
Katina

Made in the USA
San Bernardino, CA
18 September 2019